Printed in Great Britain
by Amazon

16960316R00068